Haunted
Places
of
Yorkshire

Andy Owens

D1249209

COUNTRYSIDE BOOKS
NEWBURY, BERKSHIRE

First published 2005
© Andy Owens, 2005
Reprinted 2007

All rights reserved. No reproduction
permitted without the prior permission
of the publisher:

COUNTRYSIDE BOOKS
3 Catherine Road
Newbury, Berkshire

To view our complete range of books,
please visit us at
www.countrysidebooks.co.uk

ISBN 978 1 85306 875 1

Designed by Peter Davies, Nautilus Design
Typeset by Mac Style Ltd., Scarborough, N. Yorkshire
Produced through MRM Associates Ltd., Reading
Printed by Cambridge University Press

*All material for the manufacture of this book was sourced
from sustainable forests.*

·Contents·

Haunted Places of Yorkshire

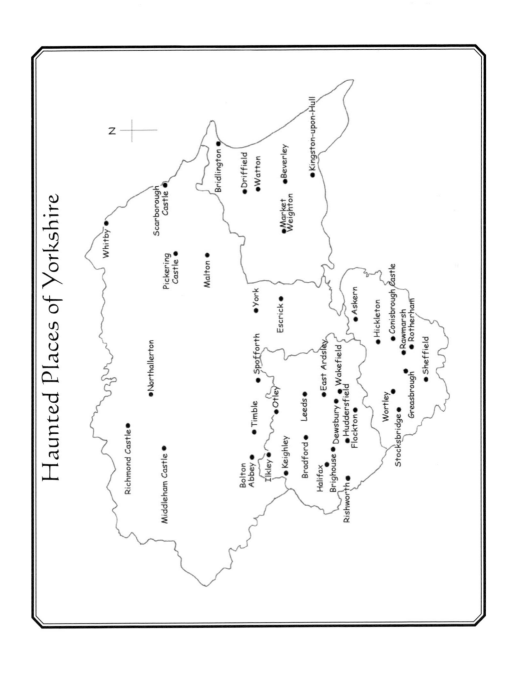

• Introduction •

Browse through any volume on British ghosts and you will no doubt discover that Yorkshire ranks as one of the most haunted counties in Great Britain. But is this so surprising? In a region that has borne witness to battle and bloodshed, poverty and disease, love and romance, it seems fitting that Yorkshire has retained permanent ghostly traces of its ancestors who lived, worked, fought and died here.

It is a sobering thought that in a world dominated by technology and apparent universal knowledge, there still appear to be areas of human experience that remain untapped and unclassified, walking the uncertain line between fact and fantasy where even almighty science fears to tread. Like the spectres of Yorkshire, I have also haunted its cities, towns and villages in the course of my research. Concentrating on modern accounts of paranormal happenings, I have combed library and newspaper archives, interviewed local people who have kindly recounted their personal experiences, and spoken to the owners, tenants and curators of many properties that are well acquainted with ghosts. *Haunted Places of Yorkshire* is an opportunity to escape the hustle and bustle of this busy, self-assured world, to explore the darkened corridors, cobwebbed attics and spooky stairwells of these chilling locations.

Spare a moment to stand alone and in silence, breathing in the past – and maybe, just maybe, you will catch a brief glimpse of a scene long forgotten: an errant knight in search of adventure and glory; a ghostly grey lady gliding effortlessly down a corridor; a phantom monk kneeling in silent prayer; or perhaps even a modern spook in a factory smock or pin-striped suit.

I hope that you will enjoy reading this book as much as I have enjoyed putting it together. And, if any of you have seen a ghost – perhaps even rubbed shoulders with an apparition featured within these pages – then please drop me a line, care of my publishers, as I would love to hear from you.

In the meantime, good ghost-hunting!

Andy Owens

DEDICATION

To Julie, Jodie, Conner and Brandon. And for Chris Ellis, who took many of the photographs, and drove me to numerous spooky locations, and for all the years of great friendship.

•West Yorkshire•

BRADFORD

Mrs Ruth Booth and her family lived in a house in the Heaton area of Bradford for nearly 28 years with Fred – their 'something'.

They moved into the house in Bridgwater Road in early 1962 and within a very short time things started to happen. The toilet would flush in the middle of the night and there was always a creak on the stairs at 2.40 am as if someone was walking up them, and then another creak at 3.20 am as if someone was walking down.

Mrs Booth kept a glass dish in the bathroom because her husband used to smoke and had the habit of dropping his cigarette ends into the toilet. One day she found that the dish had flown off the window ledge into the bath and smashed. When she replaced it with another, this also ended up in the bath making a loud bang. As Mrs Booth was placing the broken pieces into the dustbin, her neighbour, who had heard the noise, asked if they were all right. She jokingly replied that a ghost must have been responsible for the breakages.

When the neighbour said words to the effect of 'Oh dear, is it still there? The people before you only stayed in the house for a year and they complained about it and the people before them were there for seven years and they had it too,' Mrs Booth found herself becoming a little shivery.

The Booth family had to get used to many unusual happenings in their new house. Lights switched on and off, doors opened and closed when no one was nearby, things moved on their own, clocks were thrown on the floor – amazingly with no damage – and the doorbell was always ringing when there was nobody there. Mrs Booth's son was small at the time and on one occasion when the doorbell rang all on its own, he said: 'Perhaps Fred has got out and wants to come back in.' Annoyed at the constant disturbance, his mother replied: 'Well, for God's sake, Fred, come in and let us have some peace!' The ding-dong stopped immediately and the bell never rang again without there being a human finger on it.

Another incident involved a cousin's daughter who had flown from Canada to stay with the Booths. The first morning she was there she thanked Mrs Booth for tucking her in the previous night, remarking, however, that she had been cocooned so tightly at 3 am that she could hardly move! Needless to say, no one in the family had been anywhere near their guest's bed.

When Mrs Booth's son was about five or six years old, he called out to his mother one night and asked if he could have his light on as there was a funny old man sitting on his bedroom chair alongside the far wall. Mrs Booth switched on the light, saw that there was no one there, and actually sat in the chair for a while before turning off the light again, but her son said the man was still there. He described him as small and thin with hunched shoulders, a belted beige raincoat, and a hat like his granddad used to wear (a trilby) though his granddad did not match the description, as he had been a tall man. The boy slept with the light on for weeks after that.

Other people saw the little old man too. Mrs Booth's daughter was aware of him sitting watching her whenever she was in the bathroom – and visiting relatives noticed him from time to time, although this was only mentioned years later, long after the family had moved out of the house in December 1989.

In January 2003, when Mrs Booth went to an uncle's funeral in Northallerton, one of her cousin's grown-up daughters told her how she had been dozing in the bath one evening at the house in Bridgwater Road, but on opening her eyes she saw that the bathroom wall had apparently disappeared, and sitting in a chair not far away

The hidden cemetery in Shipley, near Bradford.

was a little old man, who was there one minute and gone the next! The description she gave all those years later perfectly matched that given by Mrs Booth's son.

* * *

There is an old cemetery in Shipley, just outside Bradford, that is no longer in use. It is completely hidden from view behind a bank of trees on Briggate, near the railway. In June or July 2002, Mrs Kathleen Cliff's 13-year-old daughter took a friend, who wanted to look around it, to the cemetery but when the girl returned home she was white-faced and frightened. She told her mother how a man had appeared in front of her wearing strange clothes and a medallion-type chain around his neck. Then he vanished.

Mrs Cliff wonders if this may have been the ghost of a former Lord Mayor of Bradford, if indeed such a person had been buried in the cemetery. Her daughter, unsurprisingly, has not revisited the cemetery since that day.

BRIGHOUSE

Although several counties in England lay claim to possessing the final resting place of legendary outlaw Robin Hood, West Yorkshire is thought to be one of the most likely locations, as several of the places popularly associated with the folk-hero exist near the town of Brighouse.

The grave of Robin Hood stands clearly marked for all to see – albeit on private property on the Armytage family estate in Kirklees.

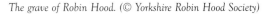

The grave of Robin Hood. (© Yorkshire Robin Hood Society)

Although some of the ghostly phenomena forms part of the ancient folklore of the area and may be explained as mere superstition, actual experiences have continued into recent years.

Judith Broadbent, a journalist for the *Dewsbury Reporter*, was granted access to the graveside, accompanied by a photographer from the newspaper. While Ms Broadbent was walking around the grave, she heard the sound of heavy footsteps approaching her, although there was no one to account for them, and she was suddenly pulled violently to the ground. She cried out 'Get Away!' – at which the force ceased and she was able to scramble to her feet.

In 1963, without permission from the owner, two men took a stroll up to the grave and saw a white-robed figure appear from nowhere and move silently before them. In 1972 one of the two, Roger Williams, returned for another sly visit with a friend and saw the same figure, which this time stopped just a few yards away from the men. They were able to describe it as a woman wearing a long white dress with a square neck and long sleeves – this was later discovered to be the type of garment worn by the Cistercian nuns who were formerly resident at the nearby abbey.

Following this sighting, the two men heard strange bangings and knockings emanating from nowhere, and it was these sounds, rather than the appearance of the apparition, that made Roger Williams vow that 'not even wild horses would drag me up there again'.

DEWSBURY

Heath Farm, on the busy Dewsbury to Wakefield road, is thought to date back to the 17th century and is constructed over a network of mining tunnels. Although there are vague tales of previous owners having experienced some paranormal activity here, a vast number of happenings were reported by Jackie and Graham Johnson who moved into the property in 1991. Although not

Heath Farm is built over a network of mining tunnels.

a medium, Jackie believes herself to have natural psychic abilities and she has sensed the presence of several spirits on the farm.

An elderly woman is sometimes seen standing in the farmyard feeding chickens from her apron, but she appears not to be the most welcoming of hostesses – for Jackie thinks she is responsible for turning off the oven just before guests are due to arrive for dinner!

A corner of the farm workshop is the favoured sitting place for an old man who has been blamed for switching off lights and machinery at exactly 3.30 pm every day. On one occasion, workers from a double-glazing company who were busy in the workshop were spooked by the man, who appeared from nowhere and sat watching them work, particularly when he disappeared when approached by one of the fitters.

Among the other phenomena reported here are a man with a shotgun who stalks the perimeter of the property; a group of children thought to be plague victims; a woman who cries for her child in the kitchen; poltergeist activity in the office, with objects such as keys, pens and money disappearing and reappearing at regular intervals; a ghostly voice which calls people's names for no apparent reason and a phantom echo voicing such phrases as 'call the dog' or 'call the horse', which are heard rebounding across the farmyard.

A doppelganger is also at work here. The couple's dog Sassy was clearly seen to be bounding across the fields away from the farm even though she was sitting quite happily next to the door of the farmhouse a second later.

Although the ghosts have startled the couple and some of their employees and visitors they are not thought to be evil, and Jackie and Graham feel they would miss them if they ever vacated the premises to haunt anyone else.

EAST ARDSLEY

In September 1993 East Ardsley Conservative Club became the unlikely setting for a ghost story as a phantom figure was clearly captured on their CCTV camera.

Bill Hodgson, the club's treasurer, was alone in the building one afternoon waiting for a friend who had arranged to meet him there, when he glanced at the camera's screen. Standing by the main doorway of the club was a man whom he did not recognise. However, Mr Hodgson assumed it was his friend and went to greet him, but nobody was there. Bemused, he returned to the screen and found that the mystery man was still standing in the doorway.

A few days later, at the same time of the afternoon, the image was seen yet again and on investigation the man was not there. Both images were recorded on video and although many people have examined the footage, they have been unable to come up with any explanation to account for the phenomenon.

Several club members recall feeling a spooky sensation in the club, which made them feel uneasy, as if someone was on the premises with them when they thought themselves to be the only people in the building.

According to Bill Hodgson: 'Some club members think it is a ghost, whereas others think it is a load of hogwash. But I'd like to see those who don't believe come in here at midnight on their own and watch the video.'

FLOCKTON

G hosts and hauntings are among the inexplicable phenomena that are alleged to be in abundance at locations criss-crossed by ley lines – ancient channels of energy, situated in the ground. It is believed by many people that the village of Flockton, south-west of Wakefield, is one such location.

Several people in Flockton have tales to tell, including a local policeman who has had odd experiences on his beat during the middle of the night. He has seen strangers pass him in the darkness and – wondering who they are as he knows they are not local – has turned round to make sure they are not up to no good, only to find that they have vanished.

The landlord and landlady of the George & Dragon have run this friendly local since the mid 1970s. Immediately after moving in they did some renovation work on the building and they think that something may have been disturbed in the process.

One particular incident, which remains etched firmly in their memories, occurred just before winter, about twelve months after they had taken over the premises. The couple had put the fire on at

Who are the strangers who pass along these streets in Flockton after dark?

lunchtime in the lounge upstairs to get it warm in time for their afternoon break and had retired there at about 3.30 pm, after the bar closed. They sat down with their coffee and sandwiches to put their feet up for a while and watch TV. The lounge door opened on its own and shortly after closed again – and, despite the fire having been on for some time, the room became icy cold.

The landlord leapt up and searched the building for a possible intruder but there was no one there but themselves. The couple sat there discussing what they had experienced for quite a while, wondering what it was that seemed to have joined them, then the lounge door opened and closed again and the icy feeling just vanished. Again the landlord checked for intruders and again there was no sign of anyone.

The George and Dragon at Flockton.

'Whatever it was', explained the landlord later, 'had obviously joined us in the room and then left soon after. We never did find an explanation for it.'

On another occasion, his wife screamed out loud one night and said she had seen a man in 18th century clothing standing on the landing upstairs, but when the landlord went to look there was no one to be seen.

Another evening, at the end of the evening session, one of the regulars in the pub said that he could see a man standing in the top room, which leads just off the bar. The landlord was sceptical, saying there couldn't possibly be anyone there, as there was no one other than the small group in the pub and all the doors were bolted. They laughed it off as they sat in the bar, but a few minutes later the man said he could see the figure again. This time the landlord went to investigate, but could see nothing. His friend had described the figure as a man dressed in 18th century clothing.

A different regular was sitting with the landlord on another occasion after the bar had closed, and told him that he had just seen two people walk past the doorway of the pub. The landlord said there was no one in the car park and dismissed the sighting with a laugh. A few minutes passed, and his friend said: 'There they are again. Two people have just walked past the door.' The landlord went to investigate, but returned saying that there was no one in sight. The regular, who was a well-built businessman and unafraid of most things, insisted the landlord accompany him to his car as he left!

HALIFAX

Formerly used as the visitors' centre for Webster's Brewery, Long Can was converted in 1987 from a row of cottages designed by the yeoman clothier James Murgatroyd in the mid-17th century. Some years ago, having heard about ghostly goings-on there, I made an enquiry to the brewery's head office and was put in touch with Ms Sarah Thornton, the then catering manageress, who turned out to be one of several witnesses to the occurrences.

Ms Thornton had heard footsteps walk around the function room during bank holidays when she knew she was the only person in the building. In fact, she had been so spooked by this that she insisted on a security guard accompanying on her rounds.

Further enquiries revealed that the bar manager often felt that he was not alone in the bar area and cellar. There were no footsteps or voices or bumps or bangs – just the unnerving sense that someone was standing close when there was no one there, or the sudden draught that we sometimes experience when someone has dashed past.

Long Can, Halifax.

The cleaners, too, talked of feeling a distinct presence in the bar area, the toilets and the museum part of the building, where a number of artefacts found in the row of cottages prior to renovation were displayed.

The catering manageress herself had the scary experience of seeing – quite clearly – an elderly woman in grey who, bizarrely, seemed to fall and vanish through the floorboards of the museum, just as Ms Thornton spun round to confront her.

* * *

Whatever did Mr Derek Rhodes capture on video in 1973? Filming his niece's wedding from the gallery above the aisle at Southowram Wesleyan Methodist chapel, near Halifax, nothing seemed out of the

The Wesleyan Methodist chapel at Southowram.

ordinary. However, on playing back the video at a later date he saw a lady dressed in black mingling amongst the well wishers.

He made enquiries of the church steward, Mr Arthur Coates, but it seemed there was no one to account for the woman on the video. She was not a guest at the wedding and nobody who was later questioned about her could recall seeing her, or anything else unusual at the time.

If she had been visible during the wedding, she would certainly have been the subject of speculation, for she stood out like a sore thumb! Dressed in black from head-to-toe, with her face covered by a black veil, her attire was more suited to a funeral than a wedding. In addition, the woman appeared to be speaking and as she did so, she faded away in full view on film.

So who was she?

HUDDERSFIELD

Although he was the promoter for Huddersfield nightclub Ivanhoe's, Derek Parkin preferred to avoid the premises. He said: 'I don't believe in ghosts, but then I don't want to meet the ghost and be proved wrong!'

The first he knew about the resident spook was when two bouncers heard footsteps coming from the balcony, and then went to look and found nothing. They heard the footsteps a second time and investigated but again with no result. After a third time, they called the police, who attended with a dog that refused to go anywhere near the balcony. The subsequent search revealed nothing to account for the footsteps.

Later Derek Parkin and the nightclub's owner Paul Davies heard the footsteps themselves when they were together on the ground floor,

The Grand Picture Theatre, Huddersfield, is now a nightclub.

but they too could find nothing. They contacted the previous owner, Ken Sewell, and he confirmed that the phantom footsteps had also been reported when he was working there.

The building began life as the Grand Picture Theatre, which opened on 14th March 1921 and finally closed its doors, under the name of the Grand Cinema, in the summer of 1957. Since then it has had several different uses, including a spell as a bingo hall and a disco.

One former male employee claimed that women never heard the footsteps, but a one-time cleaner, Madeline Dannatt, said that she and the cellar-man had both been aware of footsteps, also the sound of breaking glass, but they found nothing to account for either. She has also heard double doors swinging closed by themselves.

Theories abound, of course, and both a former projectionist and a customer of the bingo hall have been suggested as being responsible for the sounds, but whoever it is they seem to limit themselves to pacing up and down the balcony area where there used to be an office.

Although she could find nothing in the history of the building that seemed to relate specifically to the haunting, Mrs Dannatt did hear about the ghost of St Thomas's churchyard, on the same street, which kept people away from the spot after dark in the 1920s – though a connection between the two seems rather unlikely.

ILKLEY

The Mallard Inn on Church Street dates back to 1708 and is haunted by two female phantoms. In September 1999 Chris Bridge, the manager, reported that one ghost had been seen upstairs, while the other was said to frequent the bar area itself. Although descriptions were vague, staff all agreed on a sensation of being watched and not feeling alone in otherwise empty rooms.

The Mallard Inn, Ilkley, was once a gaol.

The building was a jailhouse in the late 17th/early 18th century and cells still exist in the lower part of the pub. The theory is that the ghost in the bar is someone trying to locate her place of imprisonment.

In addition, other strange happenings at the Mallard have been noted from time to time. Wine glasses have been found placed on the floor in a triangular formation and the hand-drier in the men's toilets keeps switching on by itself.

KEIGHLEY

There are many legends at East Riddlesden Hall, situated on the A650 Bradford–Keighley road. Ms Mariam Cherian of the National Trust told me that the Hall's ghosts include a

East Riddlesden Hall, Keighley.

murderer who is reputed to lurk in the reception area, a Grey Lady who walks through the rooms looking for her lover, a small girl in blue who weeps in a corner of the porch and a White Lady who is said to have drowned in the garden pond. There is also a child's cradle that rocks without anyone being seen to push it.

In 1963, however, there was an account of a haunting that does not seem to involve any of the known ghosts at East Riddlesden.

Mr M. Atkins, a Keighley taxi-driver at the time, was called to the Hall one December evening to pick up a lady. Sweeping up the drive, he stopped alongside the large stone porch at the entrance and got out of his cab. There were no lights on either in the porch or the grounds and he couldn't see well enough to find the bell push in the darkness, so he made his way round the side of the building and peered through one of the windows. There, he saw a lady dressed in period attire, which surprised him at first until he realised that as it was around Christmastime she was probably attending a fancy dress party.

Returning to the main door, he found it unlocked so he pushed it open and entered the reception area, which was empty. He called out but there was no reply. Eventually he became aware of the faint sound of music coming from a room along the passage and made his way towards it. Entering the caretaker's room, he found a lady (in normal office garb) waiting patiently for him to arrive to take her home in his taxi. Once the two were on their way back to Keighley, Mr Atkins mentioned the lady in period dress to the passenger. She went quiet for a moment and said: 'You must have seen our ghost.'

Mr Atkins later insisted that he still did not believe in ghosts, but he knows for certain that the lady he saw was definitely there in the Hall ...

* * *

In March 1998, a countryside council worker had a frightening experience whilst working on a renovation scheme at a plantation at Rivock Edge, near Riddlesden, Keighley.

David Key, a member of a drainage team, looked up to see a grey, hooded figure drift across the site, about one hundred yards ahead of him. He quickly rushed to the point where it had vanished but there was no sign of it. He commented that no human could have moved in that fashion, as it floated several feet off the ground – which he found quite terrifying.

However, when Mr Key reported what he had seen to a newspaper, a colleague, Malcolm Leyland, came forward with details of his own experience, six months earlier in September 1997. He had also seen something float across the path in front of him while he was working. He said he had never mentioned it to anyone for fear of ridicule and, although he remained very sceptical about ghosts, he was adamant that he saw something other worldly that day.

The old packhorse route which passes over Rivock Edge has witnessed many travellers over the years. (© John Riley)

Perhaps this is just one more example of a ghost being 'disturbed' by building work, as the project at Rivock Edge included the resurfacing and drainage of a bridlepath that was formerly an old packhorse route and had borne the feet of many, many travellers over the years.

LEEDS

Leeds Crown Court stands on the site of various buildings, the first of which, a police station and a block of terraced houses, were constructed around 1815. A fire station was also there, though this was demolished in 1974 to make way for the present court building. There have been reports of two spooks here over the years – or, some researchers say, two conflicting descriptions of just one.

The site where Leeds Crown Court now stands has seen, amongst other buildings, a fire station and a police station.

A news item in the local paper dated May 1994 included several accounts from various employees about an elderly, balding man in a grey suit who has been spotted crouching in a corner of one of the courtrooms.

A female security guard has seen the man several times. The first occasion was when she noticed a man of this description walking towards a courtroom and, worried that he might be an intruder, she followed him. However, as soon as she stepped into the courtroom there was no sign of the man anywhere and all other entrances to the room were securely locked. It was only at this point that the security guard realised that the man had not actually opened the door to enter – instead he had passed straight through it!

A fellow security guard once saw the man in the morning as he unlocked the main entrance and was so alarmed by the experience that he refused to go anywhere near that particular area of the building, either when unlocking the doors in the morning or locking them up at the end of the day. A male cleaner also saw the man in the grey suit, bending over in the car park below the courtroom. The female security guard refuses to be perturbed by 'Fred' as she calls him and has got quite used to seeing him, though never at any particular point in the day.

Rumours of a phantom fireman were well known during the time that the fire station stood on the site though, as that spectre was reportedly dressed in full fire-fighting kit, it seems unlikely that this could be the same ghost as the present grey-suited visitor.

* * *

The City Varieties Theatre, in Swan Street, Leeds, began as the City Palace of Varieties and before that, as so many theatres and music halls, it was the singing-room of an inn.

There is a network of underground passages here, some of which run for several miles, including one that is said to lead to Kirkstall Abbey three miles away. Among an assortment of reported phantoms at the theatre, two of the better known are a female singer and a male pianist.

TV producer Len Marten visited the theatre to watch a revue being performed there, and retired to the bar for a drink after the performance. When the bar closed for the evening, Len went to the cloakroom to fetch his coat but the lights were suddenly switched off and he was left there in complete darkness. As he slowly tried to make his way back to the bar area, he found the lights had gone out there too, and all the doors had been locked from the outside. Although he shouted to the other drinkers, they did not hear him as they chatted to themselves, descending the stairs of the theatre.

In the bar there was a coal fire burning, so Len made his way towards it and then, not knowing what else to do, settled down to sleep on a long seat that was positioned in front of the grate.

The City Varieties theatre.

After a while, he suddenly awoke and realised that the room had become intensely cold. Sitting up, he was shocked to see a lady in a crinoline dress standing beside the fire and looking directly at him. As he cried out, the woman turned to the fireplace and faded away through it, and the room suddenly warmed again. Len later testified that the woman had appeared solid, exactly like a real person – which had added to the shock when she disappeared through the fireplace. Worse still, he had to stay put in the pitch-darkness, and was not until the early hours of the morning that the night watchman found him there and let him out of the building.

Recently Jim McNish told the magazine of the paranormal *Fortean Times* about something which had happened to him at the City Varieties theatre some 20 or so years ago in June 1983, while he was a 17-year-old student studying for an A level in Stage Design. As part of the course, Jim and three other students and their teacher were to be taken on a tour of the theatre, their guide being an employee who had worked there for some 40 years and knew the place inside out.

Says Jim: 'He delighted in telling us stories about the many ghosts who haunted the theatre, including a red-haired female saxophonist who killed herself backstage after her boyfriend had dumped her and a chap who would regularly walk through a wall where a door had been bricked up many years before.

'At the back of the auditorium, between the lighting operator's booth and the entrance to the bar, was a door with a heavy padlock on it. When I asked what was behind the door our tour guide told me that there was an "evil" ghostly presence in there and none of the theatre's employees would set foot in that room. Naturally, I asked if I could go in.

'He reluctantly agreed and handed me a huge bunch of keys, pointing out the correct key to the padlock before retiring to the bar, saying he did not want to be anywhere near the door when it was opened. I unlocked the door and pulled it towards me with no feelings of trepidation. There was no light switch in the room, but missing slates in the roof allowed plenty of light to stream in from the bright summer's day outside. I could see that the floorboards had rotted away leaving about a three foot drop to floor level. A ladder had been propped up from the floor into the rafters just by the door, but the room was otherwise empty and had obviously been unused for many years.

'I stepped onto the ladder and climbed two rungs. As I looked up into the rafters I suddenly felt incredibly cold. My guts flip-flopped like I was on a roller coaster, all my hair stood on end and my heart started pumping at 200 bpm. I could not get out of that room quickly enough!

'As I leaped back into the auditorium I expected my classmates to jeer and laugh, but they looked almost as pale as I did and agreed that they had felt something weird when I was in the room, but obviously not to the same extent that I had. I have often wondered whether I really was feeling a ghostly presence or whether it was a psychosomatic reaction to the old man's ghost stories or whether there is some more mundane answer.

'One thing I do know is that I have often said to myself that I would like to revisit the City Varieties theatre in Leeds to see if I would get the same feeling again, but somehow I never seem to get round to it.'

* * *

Mrs Maureen Howley-Aylward had some odd experiences in her former home in Dawlish Avenue, Leeds 9, where she went in the 1970s as a bride with her husband John.

'I always felt that there was someone in the wings, as it were,' she remembers. 'I would be working at the sink in the kitchen and feel that someone was standing in the doorway to the stairs, which led off from the kitchen. I never, ever felt afraid in that house. On the contrary, I felt that whoever was living there with us was a good person. I would be in a room and feel that someone had come into the house, but then think maybe I heard someone next door. I would see shadows now and again, but thought that perhaps I had just imagined it.

'I had to go out to work, but always had to do things which fitted in with the domestic scene. I took a job that meant working during the night. It was in a club and sometimes I did not get in from work until four o'clock in the morning. One of my sisters would stay to take care of our son and she would sleep in the attic with him.

'One night, at around 4 am, a taxi dropped me off at home. There were Lego toys scattered in the front room, which I picked up and put in a plastic box used for that purpose. Still carrying the box, I walked through the kitchen and headed for the stairway leading up to the bedrooms. There were no lights on the stairs, though the dawn was beginning to filter through a window and out onto the landing.

'When I looked upwards, I saw a figure standing on the landing and presumed it was my husband.

'I said, "What are you doing, John?" and continued up the stairs but when I reached the top the figure had gone. Standing there for a moment, I suddenly felt someone pushing me up against the wall. Whatever or whoever it was did not touch me, because the pressure was coming from the plastic toy box I held in front of me, as though someone was pushing that into my stomach.

'My husband must have woken and I heard his voice coming from the bedroom. He was in bed! I completely lost it, screamed, threw down the toy box and ran downstairs tripping over the Lego toys, which came clattering down after me.

'Trying to reconstruct what had happened I realised that when I had looked up the stairs and thought my husband had got out of bed, I did not see his clothes. What I saw was simply a figure and I presumed it was him. When I was pressed against the wall, it did not seem to be a violent movement, just a steady pressure. I don't know how long all this lasted, but my immediate terror and flight were instinctive and I always regret having acted that way.

'I have no explanation for any of this but I am absolutely positive of one thing. From that moment on I never felt a presence in the house again and I knew that whoever it was had gone. For a long time afterwards, I would sit on those stairs and say "I'm sorry that I was afraid of you, please come back" – but it had gone. I never felt a shadow pass me in that house again.'

OTLEY

Staff at the British Heart Foundation charity shop at Otley have found that there is a mischievous spirit at work on the premises. In April 1999 the manager, Mrs Angela Harrison, told a local newspaper that at start of business on four different occasions pictures had been found with their glass fronts smashed, although there was never any sign of a break-in and nothing had been reported missing.

One of the dummies in the shop window also has a habit of turning round during the night – not all the way round, but just a little to the right – and yet when the staff leave the premises in the evening every dummy is facing forward.

There are also odd smells such as pipe tobacco noticeable in certain parts of the shop and often sounds on the shop floor when there is no one in the vicinity to account for them.

Not so long ago, workmen who were making some changes to the cellar said they were unhappy about being down there, protesting that 'there is something "not quite right" about the cellar'. They didn't see anything, but had the strong feeling that they were not alone; that unseen eyes were watching them.

Ms Linda Harrison, who also works at the shop, said that it would

The charity shop in Otley.

be great if their non-paying tenant could do something really useful, by helping to move the stock to the shop floor overnight, in time for the following day's trade!

RISHWORTH

G reenfield Lodge is a large Georgian house, which has also been called the Red House and Parkfield Hall in its time. Odd things happen on both the inside and outside of this property, which has fifteen bedrooms and a courtyard with a barn and stables. Strange sounds such as a woman's muffled voice, a car pulling up outside when there are no vehicles in the vicinity, the smell of fish and chips coming from the corner of the living room and mystery bumps and crashes from unoccupied rooms upstairs, as if someone is moving about, are regularly experienced at the Lodge.

These days cows are kept and the Lodge has its own milk supply, but previously a lady used to come and deliver it every morning.

One day as she drove up to the house she felt distinctly uneasy – she had the weird sensation that there was someone sitting alongside her in the Landrover. When she stopped, she watched with horror as her passenger door opened and closed again as if someone had climbed out of the vehicle!

One night, the owners of the Lodge were woken by the screech of brakes on the road outside. When they peered out they saw a lady sitting in a car and a man, the driver, checking the fastenings on the gate. The owners heard the woman shriek: 'Come on, let's get out of here!' She then pointed towards the Lodge and said to the man, 'It came from in there!'

The man quickly climbed back into the car, and the two sped off never to be seen again. The owners often wondered exactly what the couple had experienced and, particularly, what the 'It' was to which they had been referring.

On the night that the owners had moved in, they had brought a trailer-load of furniture, which they had left unloaded in the forecourt. The man was awoken in the early hours of the next morning by the sound of children shouting and singing. Peering through the curtains, he saw a group of youngsters running around playing in the forecourt, completely ignoring the trailer of furniture. He watched them as they moved away towards the nearby Brown Cow Inn, then again to the gate of a neighbouring farm, then returned to the forecourt and slowly faded away.

Whenever any structural alterations are undertaken at the Lodge, a ghost in a high-necked blouse with a row of buttons down the front and a long grey skirt, thought to be a previous owner, Elizabeth Emmett, appears – and she is always seen to be weeping uncontrollably.

It is not known whether this sad ghost is also responsible for the other happenings at the Lodge. Is it Elizabeth Emmett who makes the kitchen door open and close of its own accord, with the distinct sensation of someone walking through the living room, and is she the woman who has been seen going upstairs and has been mistaken for a real person more than once?

WAKEFIELD

In November 2002 Del Horler, the former landlord of the boarded up Grove Inn, on Thornhill Street in the city centre, warned builders that they might upset the resident ghost when they moved in to convert the old pub into student bedsits. Mr Horler and his family claim to have shared their home with the ghost throughout their tenancy in the 1980s.

Said Mr Horler: 'Our ghost, "Fred", does not like change. Although he is not a malicious spirit he will not be happy when building work begins, especially after all this time on his own. Soon after we moved in strange things started to happen to my wife, my children and myself.

'The range of phenomena included doors locking themselves without the use of the key and the old bell on the bar ringing on its own when there was no one in the area. I think Fred was just trying to make his presence known to us and he obviously didn't like the changes we were making.

'In one instance, during a darts-and-dominoes evening, a buffet had been organised for the players and the empty plates were strewn all over the bar. However, a large clattering sound brought the teams to a standstill and when everyone turned round they found that the untidy array of plates had stacked themselves up into a neat pile on the end of the bar!'

Mr Horler's daughter, Nicola, was terrified of sleeping in one particular room. 'It was terrible trying to get to sleep in there,' her father remembers. 'The dogs would never go in and it would suddenly go very cold for no reason. A lodger we took on also refused to sleep in there after a few chilling experiences. We weren't really scared when things like this started to happen. In fact, my children even used to talk to Fred. I don't think he is a bad spirit but he doesn't like it when his territory is threatened.

'He seemed to settle down after a while when he got used to us and we regarded as him being somewhat friendly after that. I hope that the new inhabitants learn to live with him in harmony as we all did.'

Paranormal investigator Steve Jones was among those who advised Wakefield councillors to be cautious about the renovation of the pub premises. In the late 1980s workmen had told Mr Jones that they had been doing some conversion work in the cellar when all their tools suddenly started flying around on their own. 'Poltergeists are traditionally thought to feed off energy,' he warned. 'Students especially spark off a lot of sexual energy … It would be like charging up a battery!'

In February 2003 a distressed woman, Brenda Howard, contacted the *Wakefield Express* to say she thought that the ghost of the Grove Inn was her late father, who died of a blood clot at the age of 52. Fred Couch had been was the chief maltster at the pub and had died there in 1960, when Brenda was just a girl. She wonders why the pub had to close because she believes that this is where her father's spirit was most happy – in life and in death – and he should therefore be allowed to remain in peace there.

She told the newspaper: 'I can feel how upset he is getting. He died when I was twelve and his spirit has lived in the pub ever since. We used to live next door but we had to move when they wanted to expand the pub. My father loved going in there and people would always ask him to sing songs. That's where his heart was. He hates change and he will hate it when these flats are built.'

Brenda, her husband, also called Fred, and their two grown-up children, all believe that Fred's spirit will live on.

Brenda added: 'It's never been questioned. My mum Ivy knew it too. We all did. Straight after he died, the landlady of the pub, Stella Hudson, could feel him, so she put up a plaque saying "There's always room for Fred at this inn." I'm so scared he's going to be homeless. Where will he go now? He'll be all alone and it really upsets me to think about it. Why can't they keep it as a pub so he won't be lonely?'

The plan to convert the Grove Inn to student bedsits may result in Fred causing more disturbances at the former pub, as he has done during previous renovation projects. But then who could blame him?

* * *

Mrs Hazel Wainwright (née Greenwood) was born in 1978, in a house on Brandy Carr Road, in Kirkhamgate, Wakefield. She told me: 'I have always been psychic and have known when things were going to happen, although you don't realise it as a child. Every morning, after my mum and sister had got up, I would hear someone climbing up and down the stairs, with the letterbox rattling on its own at times. One morning I was so distressed by it that I just screamed until my mum came up to see what was wrong. She hadn't heard a thing.

'I got so scared prior to moving house that I shared a bed with my elder sister. I thought I was going mad as no one else ever mentioned hearing it. However, only recently, did I learn that my father had also heard the same sounds, but didn't tell me at the time.

'We were convinced that the house was, and may still be, haunted. Even now when I pass the house, a cold shiver runs down my spine. I don't think I would ever want to return there.'

•North Yorkshire•

BOLTON ABBEY

B olton Abbey, founded in 1151, is the location of one of the oldest ghosts in Yorkshire – an Augustinian canon – and the sightings are well documented. The Reverend James Macnab, the rector here during the First World War, was asked for a written account of the haunting by none other than King George V, and many successive rectors and their families have borne witness to the phantom who haunts the church, the abbey ruins and the rectory, the latter standing on what is thought to have been the original gatehouse.

Bolton Abbey.

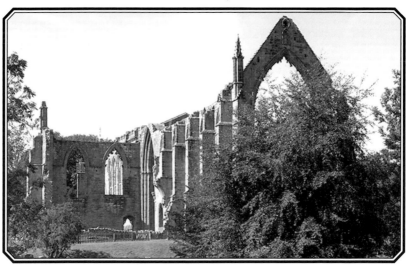

In 1912 the Marquis of Hartington, who was staying at the rectory as a member of a hunting party, was one of the first known people to have seen the apparition of a bright-eyed elderly man of around 65 years of age, dressed in a long robe with a tall pointed hood. The figure gave the impression of being as solid as you or I – not transparent like some ghosts – and appeared at close-range to the Marquis on the landing outside his room one night. So normal-looking was he that later sightings of this man have often assumed him to be a modern-day clergyman ... except that he suddenly vanishes.

There seems to be some mystery as to whether the canon appears in two different guises at different times – or if there are two separate ghosts haunting the grounds. The second mode of dress, which consists of a black cassock-like robe, black cloak and, sometimes, a flat, black hat, is seen less often, but this figure is referred to as the 'spectral black canon'. The canon who appeared to the Marquis has been nicknamed 'Punch' by later witnesses, on account of his likeness to the Punch and Judy puppet. He is still seen today by many visitors, usually in the summer months.

Lynn, the daughter of the present rector, the Reverend Griffiths, has seen the canon many times, often accompanying congregations along the path to the church. However, when the churchgoers have been questioned later, they have not been able to recall seeing the ghostly monk as they walked. A strange phenomenon indeed, that a ghost can appear in close proximity to a group of people, and the only person to see it is someone standing at a distance, while those nearby are completely unaware of it.

The canon is more often than not seen walking peacefully amongst the ruins. On one occasion, he was even run over by a visiting truck-driver who was reversing his vehicle into the rectory's driveway. The rector witnessed the incident out of his bathroom window and, convinced that he had seen a real person, rushed down to inform the driver about what he had done. The two men hurriedly checked beneath the lorry and of course there was no sign of the monk anywhere!

Mary, the rector's wife, and several guests have spotted the canon in many different places throughout the rectory. He is never frightening, just a peaceful, smiling spirit who seems happy to be there. She is convinced, however, that there is more than one ghost, all with a religious connection – she refers to them as the 'holy fathers' – and all dating from different periods in the abbey's history. One day, she even saw two figures walking together across the very room in the rectory in which she was sitting, and they vanished through the wall at a point where it is seven feet thick!

Ghostly figures have also made occasional appearances in the Old Choir section of the church, not to mention the sound of an unseen choir singing – and the faint strains of organ music have been heard from outside the church when the building is locked up and the only key is firmly in the rector's pocket.

ESCRICK

A female phantom – or rather her top half – causes quite a stir when she appears to male staff and guests, often late at night, at the 19th century Parsonage Country House Hotel at Escrick, near York. The former country residence of the vicar of Escrick has a long and interesting history, though the identity of the ghost remains a mystery.

One of the most spectacular sightings was reported in August 1998, and occurred in the hotel grounds in broad daylight during a private party. Hotel porter Wilf Bellamy described the ghost as literally floating right across the garden and straight through the guests! However, only the men saw her. Said Mr Bellamy: 'It was funny to see all them just standing there with their mouths gaping open, while the women carried on as usual.'

MALTON

The ghost of a hooded old man haunts the two hundred year old Blue Ball pub at Malton. Research has revealed that there used to be an alehouse on the same site as long ago as the 1200s, and it was used by monks from Kirkham Priory. Among many theories about the ghost is the suggestion that it might be Friar Tuck, who lived at the priory in the 1350s.

Helen Richardson, who runs the pub with her partner Steve Dobbs, reported seeing the old man in 1999. He was sitting in the bar area one evening as she was going downstairs to get ready for work. 'As I

The Blue Ball at Malton.

reached the bottom of the stairs,' she remembered, 'I could see an old man sitting in the bar. I stopped dead in my tracks and my first thought was how had he got in, because he seemed to be a real person. He looked a bit like a monk with a cloak and hood over his head and he was just sitting there, with his hands on his lap, staring straight forward. After a short while, he just faded away.' Helen just ran back upstairs and avoided going downstairs on her own for some considerable time afterwards.

Local legend states that the cellar is also haunted by the spirits of a man and woman. Helen and Steve have been aware of 'something as fine as cobwebs' brushing the face of anyone descending the steps 'when there isn't anything there'. As Helen said, with feeling: 'It's spooky.'

MIDDLEHAM CASTLE

Many castles have a history of spooky goings-on through the ages, with headless coachman and grey ladies and an assortment of other ghosts stalking the battlements and pacing the ruins.

Middleham Castle, however, is apparently devoid of these cobwebbed myths and legends – the only known experiences date from the last twenty or so years, running up to the present day.

Since the early 1980s members of the Society of Friends of Richard III, which organises frequent trips to the castle, the birthplace of this notable English monarch, have seen and sensed many odd things at the site.

In 1991 Ms Mannie Norman, secretary of the group, was walking amongst the ruins one night during May bank holiday when she heard faint 'old-fashioned' music, though from which specific direction it was coming she was not sure. When she reported what she had heard, the Reverend John Denning, honorary chaplain to

Middleham Castle.

the society, and several other members spent a night wandering around the castle and were aware of the same music coming from the chapel, which was locked up and unoccupied at the time.

Later that summer, the Reverend Denning was told by a 10-year-old boy how he and a friend had been playing in a field outside the castle walls when a knight on a horse appeared from nowhere before charging straight at them – and then through them!

The sightings of this phantom soldier, the sound of horses' hooves and swords clashing, poltergeist activity in the visitors' portacabin, and the mystery glowing light which appears amongst the ruins are among the many other phenomena reported at the castle, which as I write are due to be investigated by a number of paranormal research groups.

NORTHALLERTON

Just outside Northallerton, there is a slip road which connects the villages of Yafforth and Romanby. It is a simple, modern tarmac thoroughfare, probably a fairly recent development, and a less spooky location would be hard to find! And yet, the experiences related to me by one person on this road, on a bright sunny afternoon, are spine-chilling.

A young lady from Grassington often cycles down the road during the summer months, when she visits a friend in Northallerton. One afternoon in June a few years ago, the two friends took this lane as a short cut and cycled straight into what they later agreed was a 'weird and brooding atmosphere'.

My correspondent recalled how both she and her friend seemed to be overcome with a peculiar feeling at exactly the same time. They suddenly became dizzy and disorientated, and had to stop by the kerb for a minute or two to get their bearings. Eventually, after a few minutes, the sensation gradually abated. At the time, they thought it strange that they should both be affected at the same time, but it was not until they returned home that they sat down and discussed it.

The lady told me that her friend knew a gentleman of Northallerton, who had experienced a similar feeling of dizziness and disorientation, and, worried that it might be an early symptom of an illness, he quickly made an appointment to see his doctor. After a full check-up, however, he was informed that nothing was amiss.

They saw no phantom figures nor heard unearthly voices or sounds, but both felt there was something very real, of one form or another, present on that lane. Both women and their male acquaintance agreed that the sensation was not frightening or alarming - just strange. It has not kept them away from the lane since their experiences and it has never again been repeated.

Just who or what it is that lingers in the shadows, we don't know and, despite appealing for further information through local newspapers, I have received nothing from any other witnesses about this intriguing phenomenon. So, is this just a one-off occurrence or have others experienced similar sensations elsewhere? And, does it even deserve to be classed as a ghostly or paranormal experience? If only one person had experienced this sensation, then we might conclude that the experience was related more to *them* than the actual *location*. However, with three witnesses over a period of two years or so, it is tempting to conclude that the slip road itself should be studied rather than the people themselves!

Perhaps a reader of this volume has experienced a similar sensation on this quiet stretch of road? If they would contact me, via my publishers, we may be able to shed some light on this mystery which, frustrating though it is, must be labelled 'unsolved'.

PICKERING CASTLE

The ruins of Pickering Castle stand on the edge of the North York Moors – and even in its present state it is a fine example of a Norman motte and bailey, built between 1069 and 1070, with stone replacing wood in the early 12th century. Pickering was strengthened many times over the years and was used to maintain control in the north, but never really

Pickering Castle.

played a major role in any major battles or sieges. Monarchs stayed there occasionally during hunting trips in the surrounding Forest of Pickering.

Despite its relatively peaceful existence, Pickering Castle has a ghost of a monk. A couple walking amongst the ruins in the early 1980s reported seeing the figure for a few seconds, arms outstretched as if he was carrying an unseen something. The monk was described as being tall with a long cloak or habit, and he was purposefully moving across the castle grounds to the keep.

RICHMOND CASTLE

Set on a cliff overlooking the River Swale, 11th century Richmond Castle stands in a dramatic position and would have posed an ominous challenge to any invaders who dared to

Richmond Castle.

attack it. However, the castle never saw military action and was almost in ruins by the 16th century.

Two ancient legends abound at Richmond. One – in common with many other castles throughout England and Wales – is connected with King Arthur; the other concerns a phantom drummer who is never seen, though the steady rhythmic beating of his drum sends shivers down the spines of local people, reminding them to stay away after nightfall.

Odd lights have been reported in the ruins during the daytime by visitors, and have also been seen during the night from outside the stronghold walls, as well as in the immediate vicinity of the castle. Whether they are candle-lights or lanterns held by a ghostly soldier – or perhaps one of the various forms of spook-lights or spirit-lights that have been reported from other locations (see also Conisbrough Castle, page 63) – is not known.

Whatever their cause or origin they are phenomena noted in previous centuries that have continued in the latter half of the 20th century. It remains to be seen, however, if they continue to be reported by visitors and locals in the 21st century.

SCARBOROUGH CASTLE

Scarborough Castle is located on a roughly triangular headland that rises three hundred feet above the sea. There is evidence of Iron Age settlements and the remains of a Roman signal station on the site, but the first medieval castle was built by William le Gros, Count of Aumale, in the 1130s, and it was taken over by Henry II in 1154. Extensive improvements were made by him and subsequent monarchs over the next hundred years.

In 1312 the castle came under a brief siege when Edward II's favourite, Piers Gaveston, fleeing retribution from the barons, took refuge there. A shortage of supplies forced him to surrender within a

Scarborough Castle.

fortnight. Despite promises of safe conduct, his journey back south was brought to an abrupt end when he was captured and beheaded by the Earl of Warwick.

Greater resistance was offered by the Royalist defenders of the castle in 1645 when they were besieged by a Parliamentary force. They managed to withstand a five-month siege, despite an artillery bombardment that had caused half the keep to collapse within just three days. After the Civil War, the castle was used as a prison and in the mid 18th century a barracks block was added that remained in use until the middle of the next century, being demolished finally as a result of shelling in the First World War.

The ghost here, according to legend, is that of Piers Gaveston, who appears as a shadowy figure darting in and out of the ruins, attempting to knock unwary visitors over the edge of the battlements.

Why, from all the people connected with the castle over so many momentous years, the ghost should be that of Gaveston remains a mystery, but it – or at least its threatening presence – is very real, as testified by a whole range of witnesses. Visitors have felt unnerved, even in broad daylight, while walking the battlements, suddenly overcome with a dreadful sense that they are not alone. When there is the added threat that something unseen is not only watching them but is ready to pounce at any moment, it is quite enough to persuade them to quicken their pace and explore other parts of the castle in haste!

SPOFFORTH

The ruins of Spofforth Castle, in the tiny village of Spofforth south-east of Harrogate, are a mere shell of their former glory. Although the foundations of the castle date from the 13th century, the majority of what remains dates from the 15th century, when major alterations were made. Rather than standing at the head of the village, overlooking the residents as many castles do, this one is in the midst of other buildings, rather forlorn and somewhat unnoticed.

Over the years people have reported seeing strange things in the castle grounds, including the blueish-white apparition of the top half of a woman who appears on the castle tower and then jumps or falls (or is pushed) to the ground below. Why only the upper portion of the woman is visible is not known, for there are no documented legends attached to the history of the castle to account for her.

Two picnickers saw this ghost in 1969, and four years later, in 1973, a teacher and a group of schoolchildren were horrified to witness the phantom suicide. They thought it was an actual person in a real suicide attempt, until the ghost disappeared just before it reached the ground, leaving the watchers shocked and relieved in equal measures!

Many local people from surrounding districts have sensed a great sense of doom and gloom while walking amongst the ruins. This impression of cold emptiness is reported to be pleasurable to some, who like to wander among the ramparts and get lost in the atmosphere of the place, whereas others are left feeling numbed and unnerved by the stillness and calmness of the castle.

Perhaps Spofforth Castle's occupants had sustained some great loss in the centuries since its completion – there is plenty of speculation but no one has been able to discover any explanation in the site's history for this eerie feeling.

Spofforth Castle.

TIMBLE

Swinsty Hall near Timble is over four hundred years old and looks like the classic haunted house from a horror film. Mr and Mrs Cuckston resided there for more than ten years and while they did not actually *see* any ghosts they are in no doubt whatsoever that the Hall is haunted.

One night Mrs Cuckston went to bed rather early while her husband was listening to some music downstairs. Shortly after, she heard someone come into the bedroom and get into bed. However, when after a few minutes she rolled over she found the other half of the bed empty and the bedclothes undisturbed, and she could still hear the sound of music downstairs where her husband was still sitting.

Other strange happenings that the couple have reported were the sounds of ghostly voices calling their first names from upstairs. When they went up to investigate they would find no one. Curiously, when they were both in the kitchen only the person who was called could hear the voice, whereas the other heard nothing at all.

When their daughter was a baby Mrs Cuckston often slept in the nursery alongside her crib, while her husband stayed in the master bedroom. One night she awoke to find herself 'almost paralysed' with coldness, a feeling she could not explain. As she was just about to climb out of bed to investigate, someone put an extra blanket over her and she settled down and went back to sleep. The next morning she awoke to find the room had returned to its original warm temperature. Downstairs, she thanked her husband for laying the blanket over her, but, bemused, he said had not left the other bedroom all night.

WHITBY

Perched prominently high on the cliff, the eastern front of Whitby's abbey dominates the skyline. The ruins we see today date almost entirely from the 1220s, after the abbey had been refounded by the Benedictine monks from Evesham. However, St Hilda, the respected abbess from the 7th century, allegedly appears in the window of the abbey on dark nights, bathed in a golden glow like an angel.

The modern haunting here though, like that of Scarborough Castle just a stone's throw down the coastline, is more of a presence, except that some people have also reported a dark figure, with the noticeable outline of a woman, shaking her head and wringing her hands as if greatly upset. Witnesses have felt inclined to approach and offer comfort, asking what is so distressing her, and have reported being surprised to find that she is dressed in old-style garments, some say from the 18th or 19th century.

Although no one has seen her actually vanish, many folk have turned their head for just a split-second only to find that the lady has disappeared in an instant They have been quite adamant that there is nowhere she could have gone to in that small space of time.

YORK

The Theatre Royal, St Leonard's Place, York was once the site of the St Leonard's Hospital which was run by nuns. Not surprisingly, the ghost here is that of a young nun who is usually seen in a small room near the dress circle of the theatre.

The casts and crews of the hundreds of plays staged at the Theatre Royal have had unaccountable things happen to them and the nun, dressed in a grey and white coif, is also seen leaning over a stage box and at the front of the auditorium.

The most spectacular sighting must surely have been during the dress rehearsals for the play *Dear Octopus* when the cast were on the stage practising their lines. The actors gradually became aware of a strange light slowly appearing in the centre of the dress circle. As they gazed, dumbfounded, the light gradually formed into a head and shoulders of what looked like a nun sitting watching the cast staring back at her. After a while the figure faded away, and after the actors had recovered they continued rehearsing. However, a few moments later the same thing happened again, but this time the ghost was less distinct as if the form was gradually losing colour and shape.

In 1965 some members of a production company attempted to rid the theatre of the spirit and formed a circle in the small room by the dress circle where odd occurrences had been noted over the years.

The Theatre Royal, York.

After a few minutes, the group gradually became aware of the sound of approaching footsteps and, suddenly, everyone present shrieked as a tall woman in a long gown walked straight through the closed door and into the room. One of the actresses became hysterical, screaming with utter fright, and upon this the apparition immediately vanished.

* * *

Mrs Susan C. Bullman relates the very strange experience of her brother Ian on a day trip to York in July 1962.

Susan was then a young girl and few years older than Ian, who was about six at the time, and remembers that they were on an outing to

York Minster.

the city with their parents. At around 4 pm the four had walked along the Roman wall and also visited the museums and gift shops, but found there was still about an hour before their train home was due, so they decided to visit York Minster.

Once inside, Ian began to lag behind his family though Susan, as a protective older sister, kept a watchful eye over him. She can still recall her mother saying how she wouldn't like to be left alone in the Minster at night because of the gloomy atmosphere. When Susan looked back at Ian, he seemed even further behind. Suddenly, he ran towards them and hid under his mother's coat, crying and obviously distressed by something.

After he calmed down, Ian said that he had seen a man running about the Minster very fast – wearing no clothes! Their father tried to make light of it, saying he would give his jacket to the man if he was naked, but there was nothing to account for Ian's strange behaviour and they all left the Minster feeling a little uneasy.

In the following years, no one ever mentioned the incident unless Ian himself brought up the subject himself, but as he grew older Ian described the man in more detail. He said the man had long black bushy hair and was darting about wildly near the altar. As he watched, Ian had become very scared. He recalled he had stood near one of the iron gates looking through to a part which had been cordoned off and it was frightening because no one else had noticed the man, even though there were other visitors there and some were looking in the man's direction, but not showing any reaction at all.

His father always tried to reassure Ian, saying that it had been a dream he had while falling asleep for a few minutes – and yet Susan had only turned away from her brother for about ten seconds, so she pointed out that he must have fallen asleep standing up!

When Ian was about ten years old, he started buying a children's magazine called *Look & Learn*. One day Susan was glancing through it when she came across an article about a man named Jonathan Martin – a lunatic who had set fire to York Minster. However, what made Susan really go cold was the fact that the man had been naked! She knew from that moment that Ian had indeed seen a ghost all those years ago. Recently she again asked Ian about his experience and he was still able to describe the incident very clearly.

Although Susan says she has never seen a ghost herself, she clearly remembers looking into the face of her brother who just had, and will never forget his expression and his genuine fright.

* * *

In the old dairy at Kirkby Hall near York there is often the smell of freshly baked bread when there is no one around to account for it, and the sound of children's feet running has been heard on the stone-flagged passageways of the ground floor, along with the rustle of silk.

Mr and Mrs Clark, former resident caretakers at the Hall, experienced a number of odd things during their time working there. However, the most curious incident sounds as if it was something like a 'crisis apparition' – a situation where someone undergoing a crisis, or often at the point of death, appears in quite another location in front of a friend or relative – rather than a ghost attached to the Hall itself.

Mrs Clark had been instructed that a lady would be coming to visit the Hall and that she was to be made very welcome on her arrival. Mrs

Clark waited and waited but there was no sign of the visitor, so she locked up and retired for the night.

At 2 am Mrs Clark was awoken by the sound of a car's engine, as it was obviously approaching the Hall up the driveway. Peering out of the window she saw a white-haired old lady get out of a car – a Standard Vanguard – and close the door with a bang. Mrs Clark opened the window to inform the visitor that the door was locked and say that she would come downstairs and let her in. However, on opening the window she watched as the old lady climbed back into the car and drove off.

The next day she received a phone call from the visitor's companion who told her that the lady could not come to visit as she had been killed at 2 pm the previous afternoon in her car – a Standard Vanguard. It was only then that Mrs Clark realised that the car that had appeared the previous night could not have entered or left the Hall grounds as the gates on the drive had been firmly closed and locked.

* * *

Like so many ghosts reported throughout the ages, the Roman soldiers seen in 1953 by apprentice plumber Harry Martindale in the cellars of the Treasurer's House in York seem to have been disturbed by renovation work to old stonework. The labyrinthine cellars below the city's streets have been the scene of several ghostly encounters with the centurions, but Harry's description of what he saw is of particular interest. The Romans appeared just a few feet from him, in procession, marching through one wall and then out of the other, and yet did not once turn to him or acknowledge his presence in any way.

Their dusty, ragged, dishevelled appearance did not match the Romans as depicted in Hollywood movies of the time, which convinced researchers that the young man was telling the truth, not to mention that fact that Martindale noted specific details about the Romans' attire which were not widely known at that time.

Four years after this now-famous encounter, the then caretaker Mrs Joan Mawson also reported sightings of Roman soldiers. On the first occasion, while walking through a low tunnel towards the cellars, she encountered a troop of Roman soldiers just two feet away from her. She subsequently saw them several times; sometimes they were on foot and other times on horseback. Like the soldiers Harry Martindale reported, they looked dirty, dishevelled, mud-splashed and exhausted. One mounted soldier was resting his head on his horse's neck as it trotted through the cellar, in an attitude of extreme tiredness.

Psychical researcher Steve Cliffe and two colleagues decided to investigate the haunting. Although they were not allowed to hold a vigil in the cellars at the time as they were in a dangerous state, they

The Treasurer's House, York.

were permitted to set up recording equipment, which was then retrieved by the group the following morning. Among the sounds recorded were that of a bugle, marching feet, the steady rhythmic beating of something like a kettledrum, and the sound of someone breathing very, very close to the microphone!

* * *

Miss Joanna Rudd, who lives a few miles outside York, replied to one of my newspaper appeals for spooky experiences and, if there were a prize for the most fascinating happening recorded in this volume, I am sure it would be reserved for her.

Says Miss Rudd: 'I am writing to tell you of an incident which happened between York and Ripon on a Sunday evening early in March 2001 at around 8 pm. I was in my final year of teacher training at Ripon & York St John's College in Ripon and, as usual, I had travelled home for the weekend. I was returning to college along the route I took each weekend, but on this particular occasion I was an hour later than usual, when the following happened.

'It was a dry clear night with no moon and my journey had been uneventful so far. I turned off the A59 onto the slip road for the A168 just past Allerton Park. The A168 was formerly part of the A1 and now runs parallel to it for a few miles between Walshford to the south and Dishforth to the north.

'As I neared the end of the slip road, I looked onto the main road to see if it was safe to turn. To my left, I saw two sets of headlights, side by side as if ready for a race. At first I thought nothing of it as I knew there was a lay-by there and thought that one car was parked in that. I noticed that the car to the left of the pair had one headlight brighter than the other.

'I waited to see if they would pass, as I had no wish to be followed by cars in a race, but they appeared to be stationary. I pulled out and set off right, towards Boroughbridge. I glanced back in the mirror and noticed that the cars had gone. This did seem strange as I had seen them both so clearly and had a good view of the stretch of road at all times, but I just thought they must have turned off onto the slip road.

'I continued up a slight incline and, suddenly out of nowhere, a car with one headlight appeared close to the back of my car. It did not speed up from behind, as the road was clear. It just appeared like someone had dropped it there.

'The car seemed quite old as it had round headlights, one shining brighter than the other, giving the car an odd appearance. The light was so intense it lit up the inside of my car and I could hardly bear to look in the mirror.

'A feeling of sadness and despair seemed to come over me that I had not previously been feeling, and I frantically tried to concentrate on listening to the radio. I started to panic as I felt the car was moving even closer and I was sure it was going to crash into me. I did try to see a driver, but the headlight proved too bright to even make out the

The slip road leading to the A168 near Allerton Park, York.

shape of a car. I braked a few times in the hopes that the driver would overtake me, but this was to no avail.

'As I climbed to the top of the hill, a point where it is possible to see the road behind clearly, the car just disappeared. As quickly as the light had appeared, it just went out. The car did not leave the road, as I would have seen the beam of light move and probably the car as well. Furthermore, on that particular stretch of road, there are no junctions, gateways or lay-bys and the grass banks quite sharply at either side.

'Throughout the whole experience, which lasted about ten minutes, although it felt like hours, no other vehicle passed me in either direction.

'I have been back along the route many times and have failed to find any reasonable explanation as to why a car that was following me so closely could just disappear so quickly. During four years of using the road regularly nothing like this had ever happened to me before or has done since.'

•South Yorkshire•

ASKERN

A ghost at the Crown Hotel in Askern, north of Doncaster, is vividly recalled by Mrs Banks, who was frightened by it as a teenager, when her parents were the licensees there.

Her bedroom was situated on the first floor, directly opposite the flight of stairs leading to the second floor, which was used mainly for the bed and breakfast service offered at the inn. However, one room – 'The Room' as Mrs Banks always referred to it – was unoccupied and

The Crown Hotel in Askern.

provided a storage area for furniture and other items. Feeling bored one day, she decided to explore this treasure trove, which looked as if it had not been opened for years. Dust covered everything, but as the room was much larger than her own bedroom she asked her parents if she could clear it out and move into it.

When they agreed, the teenager and her mother spent a lot of time removing the junk, painting the walls and cleaning the room up ready for its new occupant, and Mrs Banks remembers feeling excited at the prospect of having a new bedroom.

The teenage girl had always been a sound sleeper, but the very first time she went to bed in this room, happy with her new surroundings and tired after her exertions, something woke her up during the night. It wasn't a sound – there was no sound at all – just a distinctly uneasy feeling that someone was watching her, even though there was certainly no one else there.

Glancing towards the window, she could see the heavy drapes blocking out the moonlight and then, slowly, they opened ... She says she can still remember this happening very clearly, although it occurred many years ago, as it is etched firmly in her memory.

She recalls: 'I can see them now, slowly drawing across the window and flooding the room with moonlight. I can still hear them, the only sound in that strange atmosphere, the sound of the curtain runners on the rail, as they worked together to open the curtains.'

In a sheer panic, she rushed down from the upper floor and spent the rest of the night sitting on the bed in her old room with the light switched on until it was time to get up. In the morning, when she told her brother what had happened, he was not at all surprised and revealed that he had heard odd noises coming from the room on the second floor whenever he used the bathroom that was situated directly next door. He said it had often sounded as if furniture was being moved around, even though he knew there was no one in the room and, indeed, it was so tightly packed that movement would have been impossible anyway.

He pointed out to his sister that, even without the sounds, there was obviously something odd about the room. Hadn't she ever wondered, he asked her, why there were bars on the window and a heavy lock fitted to the outside of the door? The Crown Hotel is over two centuries old, and whoever or whatever was in that room had obviously been locked in there many years ago.

CONISBROUGH CASTLE

Although built as long ago as 1180, the castle on the edge of the South Yorkshire village of Conisbrough has had a comparatively uneventful history and, not having been connected with any notable personages or well-known battles, has

Conisbrough Castle.

managed to keep out of the history books. Its keep, however, is recognised as one of the finest and best preserved in England.

There are several ghostly residents attached to the castle, though specific identities remain vague because, as far as I am aware, there are no colourful legends, fanciful or otherwise, which have been unearthed to account for their origins. Over the years, many people have reported a plethora of paranormal activity within the castle itself, and throughout the grounds, including the sound of footsteps, unexplained lights emanating from the chapel, not to mention the figures of a White Lady on top of the keep and a Grey Monk that wanders through the ruins.

Tom Bremner recalls a visit in the 1960s when, as a youngster, he and a group of other boys spent a good few hours playing amongst the ruins, whilst their parents idled away their time on the castle green. Darting in and out of the walls, and leaping over the ancient rubble playing army games, Tom glanced up at the keep and there, for an instant, he was sure he saw a lady dressed in a long white dress. He did a double take. He recalls how she wasn't doing anything that would make one stare, but looked a little odd just gazing into the distance and quite out of place. Her long, flowing dress, too, seemed strange and showed up against the colour of the castle wall. When he glanced back a split-second later, she was gone.

Many years later, while in conversation with one of the other young boys, Jeff, now grown-up and with his own family, they moved onto the subject of ghosts and haunted houses. Jeff volunteered how he had once had a fleeting glimpse of a lady in white dress while he was on a childhood outing to Conisbrough Castle. Tom Bremner tells how he was utterly dumbfounded to realise that they had seen the same figure, possibly at the same time, from their different positions in the ruins, though neither of them had told each other, or anyone else for that matter, for nearly thirty years!

In 1987 Eileen Townsend was walking her two spaniels at the castle, when she spotted the figure of a woman outside the ruins. The woman, dressed in a distinctive black dress that seemed to pull over her head – though Eileen was sure it was not a nun's habit – was striding determinedly down the grass bank which descends from the keep.

Eileen did not see the figure for very long. She had craned her neck round one of the walls to watch the woman, so curious was her appearance, until she passed out of sight. By the time Eileen had hurried to the front of the building, the figure was nowhere to be seen.

There are also vague tales of odd lights coming from the chapel when there is nothing to account for them. Sometimes they remain stationary for some time before flickering out, while on other occasions they float from left to right – a phenomenon commonly referred to by researchers as 'spook-lights'.

In ages past these were thought by superstitious locals to be the spirits of the dead coming alive at night. Some are seen over marshlands and are now termed 'Will-o'-the-Wisp', explained as gases given off by marshes at night, but spook-lights are reported from various settings around the world, and may have different explanations for different types. Whether they are examples of genuine psychic phenomena, or optical illusions, is still open to debate, but they often appear to be controlled by some form of intelligence, remaining still for some time, before veering sharply away and returning again.

At Conisbrough, along with the sound of footsteps in the castle's keep, sightings of these lights are reported much more regularly than the apparitions.

GREASBROUGH

Phantom pedestrians wander the pavements of several South Yorkshire streets and highways causing chaos and confusion to the motorists of today. From the bend in the road at Wortley church to the notorious ghosts of Stocksbridge Bypass, these spirits have caused many a crash – some fatal.

In the Greasbrough area between 1980 and 1985, on a stretch of road known locally as The Whins, which runs south from the village of Nether Haugh, there were three incidents of motorists screeching to a halt to avoid hitting a woman who had stepped out of the shadows and into the paths of their cars.

Mrs Mary Breedon, a former worker for the Probation Service in Barnsley, watched a tall woman in white step out from a large house on the Fitzwilliam Estate, and disappear. Mrs Breedon rapidly brought the car to a halt and climbed out, and was further stunned to find no trace of the woman anywhere. When she arrived at the meeting she was due to attend that evening, a former colleague told of other experiences on that same stretch of road.

The Whins near Greasbrough.

A young man had been startled to watch the woman not only step in front of his car, but actually hit the bonnet, slam against the windscreen and disappear somewhere over the roof. When police were called to the scene an extensive search of the area revealed no trace of the victim.

In the third incident, a woman travelling in the passenger seat as her husband negotiated his car down the hill saw the woman in white appear then disappear in a split-second. Her husband, however, did not see her although he had been looking straight ahead at the time.

There are no ghostly legends attached to this stretch of road and yet these three witnesses, unknown to each other, each experienced a similar occurrence within the space of five years. As far as I know there have been no further reports of this nature – but perhaps it is only a matter of time.

HICKLETON

As I was concentrating on modern accounts of ghosts and hauntings while researching this book, I was very doubtful when I read of a phantom horse and rider at the small village of Hickleton, near Goldthorpe, because it sounds exactly like a cobwebbed old myth rather than an actual supernatural experience.

However, when I delved further into the account, written by psychic investigator Terence Whitaker, I realised that this is a ghost that, although dressed in attire of centuries past, has only been reported by motorists and pedestrians in comparatively recent years.

Terence is the author of several books on ghosts, another on the double-murderer Dr Buck Ruxton, and an award-winning play for the disabled. In addition to this, he has written and presented regional programmes for TV and radio on supernatural subjects and has investigated many hauntings in a personal capacity. He has had a few brushes with the paranormal but this one, experienced at the

The haunted junction, Hickleton.

age of sixteen, remains etched firmly in his memory as the most frightening.

Says Terence: 'In those days I lived with my grandmother in Thurnscoe and worked at Doncaster, about eleven miles away. Because I didn't finish work until after 10.30 pm and the last bus left Doncaster at 9.30 pm, I had to cycle home every night.

'Leaving Doncaster, I would cycle up the Barnsley road through Scawsby and Marr and then begin a gradual uphill climb to Hickleton. Hickleton is neighboured by coal pits but it is an island of charm really, with a fine church at the crossroads and, behind it, the seventeenth-century home of the Halifax family. Apart from that, several small cottages make up the remainder of the village.

'On this particular night, as I cycled up the tree-lined road towards the church, I could see, between the trees on my left, the

...ich would cross my path outside the church. There was very
...c along here in those days, but had anything been
...the crossroads from my left, I would have been able to
...well.

'I was surprised to see a figure on horseback, trotting in a leisurely
way towards the junction. I remember thinking to myself "What a
funny time for someone to be out on a horse," for although it was late
June and quite light, it was after 11 pm.

'The horseman came to the crossroads and stopped, looking down
the road up which I was cycling, until suddenly the horse shied and
I was able to distinguish quite clearly a billowing cape and tricorn
hat.

'That in itself was bad enough, but then to my absolute terror both
horse and rider vanished before my eyes. I was no more than fifty or
sixty yards away by this time and I think it would be an
understatement to say I was frightened, I was terrified. In fact, had I
not been so near to home I would have turned back to Doncaster. As
it was, I put my head down and pedalled furiously past the spot,
covering the last two miles or so in record time.

'Since then, while doing research for my books on ghosts, I have
had one or two other frightening experiences, but I don't think I have
ever been so terrified as I was that night in 1953.

'When I reached home and had fully recovered, I told my
grandmother of my experience, thinking she would accuse me of
being over-imaginative, but she just listened quietly and then
suggested I have a word with one of the neighbours who had been a
policeman and used to patrol that area on his bike some years
before.

'The neighbour told me that he had seen the ghost himself on one
occasion and that several people living in the village had reported
seeing it, but no one knew who it was.

'One theory was that it was the ghost of a man ambushed by troops
and killed on that spot. Research over the years has failed to bring any

fresh evidence to light, but I understand the ghost has been seen as recently as 1977 by a lorry driver, who braked hard on reaching the crossroads when a figure on a horse suddenly appeared from nowhere and vanished just as quickly.'

RAWMARSH

In December 2002 staff and students of Rawmarsh Comprehensive School told newspapers how they had experienced a range of phenomena on the premises.

Mr John Key, a clerk of works at Rotherham Council, was working at the school and reported that he had seen the apparition of a stooped man, around 5ft 6ins tall and dressed in a suit, walk straight through a wall. Officials thought it was a leg-pull at first, but later two former caretakers came forward to tell of their own similar sightings of a ghost.

An old graveyard used to adjoin the school and, as is often the case, the theory is that the spirits of the dead have been disturbed by building work carried out on the building. The old stage area of the school was being redeveloped as science laboratories and this was pinpointed as the cause of the disturbances.

When a surveyor was sent to the school to take photographs of the area, prior to work being started, he was astounded to find odd shapes on the photograph – they looked like bubbles, though there was nothing visible at the time to explain them. A spokesman for the school said that there seemed to be the images of people's faces within the bubbles, or 'orbs' as many investigators of the paranormal call them. The spokesman said: 'One has a beard, another looks like a skull. It is very weird.' The surveyor was very shaken after he examined the photographs, as was Mr Key after he saw the ghost.

Pupils of the school have often reported sightings of an extra 'classmate' in the school, one that is there one minute and gone the next.

Also, one Sunday, engineers were working at the otherv
school when they heard the distinct sound of an organ bei
Although they searched thoroughly, they could find n
account for it, and when they enquired about it the follow
they were informed that there were no organs on the school

ROTHERHAM

In 1982 miner Stephen Dimbleby had an experience he would never forget at Silverwood Colliery near Rotherham. Just beginning his shift, he trekked down the route to the part of the mine where he worked and saw a figure ahead of him. The man looked odd to Stephen, particularly when he neared him, as he was

The Silverwood Colliery, Rotherham.

dressed in old mining clothes and had an old-fashioned gas lamp.

'He looked real and solid,' Stephen explained later, 'because I couldn't see through him. He was just an ordinary bloke, and my first instincts were that it was just somebody mucking about. And then it hit me: he'd come from nowhere, just appeared. And when I shone my light in his face, there were no features on his face. And then I just dropped everything and set off running out.'

Colleagues of Stephen vouched for his sincerity as he ran from the mine, screaming and vowing never to return to the shaft, and he was given an alternative job working above the ground instead.

SHEFFIELD

Ashdell Grove is a beautifully preserved Victorian house, built in 1871 for an industrialist and originally called 'Victoria Park'. For many years it has housed the offices and studios of BBC Radio Sheffield.

Radio presenter Gerry Kersey is used to being in the studio at night and alone, and is well aware of the sounds that electronic equipment makes even when it is not being used, so he is not someone who shudders at the slightest noise. However, one night, while he walking past a cupboard on an upper floor, he was shocked to see the door swing open and its contents come spilling out in front of him. Mr Kersey was adamant that they had not merely fallen out; it looked like someone was throwing them out even though there was no one there.

Another presenter staged a ghost-hunt one night accompanied by a psychical researcher and they spent part of the night slowly walking through the building. As they approached the foot of the staircase, the researcher looked up at the top of the stairs to see a tall middle-aged man peering down at them. Suddenly, both the researcher and the presenter were overcome with a fit of violent sickness, which shot through them in waves, and it was not until they had moved away

The studios of BBC Radio Sheffield.

from that immediate area that they quickly recovered and experienced nothing else that night.

Even before the investigation got under way, the presenter knew there was something odd about the building. He had been sitting in his office one night editing tapes, when the building was otherwise empty, and he distinctly saw a dark, shadowy figure move past the circular window in the door. Springing up, he checked outside the room and looked down the corridors but could find nothing to account for the figure.

A senior producer has walked out of his studio at Ashdell Grove three times because he sensed he wasn't alone and on one occasion electronic equipment was operating by itself, for which he has since been unable to find an explanation.

Sports producer Phil Baldy had an unusual experience when he saw the face of an old man staring at him through the circular window in the outside door as he prepared to lock up for the night and he has often experienced other inexplicable phenomena such as figures out of the corner of his eye and odd noises coming from empty rooms and studios.

One young lady, who prefers to remain unnamed, often made up a bed for herself on the studio floor at night, rather than take what was a long journey home, but eventually ceased doing this because of the strong feeling that she was being watched.

Freelance reporter Richard Hemingway has heard footsteps entering the building and climbing the stairs, yet there was no one there but him, and engineer Peter Mason has found that controls in studios have been tampered with when he is the only one within reach of them.

Although there is pleasant working atmosphere in the building during the day, many of the staff know only too well that there is a presence here, watching and waiting ...

* * *

Perhaps it is not so surprising that hospitals tend to be focal points for ghostly activity, because although they are often the places where people are brought into the world, they are also the places where many spend their last moments before passing away.

Middlewood Hospital, in the suburb of Wadsley, has had a variety of purposes since it was opened as a mental asylum in 1872, including use as a war hospital and a TB sanatorium. Since being converted to a general hospital, however, various parts of the building have become 'notorious' with both staff and patients, following a huge catalogue of unexplained events.

Hospital porter Henry Gaines will never forget hearing footsteps climbing a staircase past the end of Ward 11 and actually passing him as they continued up to the next floor. He then heard the heavy double doors on the floor above swing open and shut, but on investigation he found nothing that could have caused this.

Ward Nurse Jean Higham was on night duty and was sitting at her desk in Ward 8 when she saw an elderly patient climb out of bed and start walking towards the doors at the other end of the ward. Jean set off after her, wondering if the lady was all right, and was startled to see the 'patient' suddenly turn and disappear straight through the wall! The next morning she mentioned the incident to her relief nurse and although her colleague said nothing, Jean was treated to an expression which implied: 'Oh no, not again.' When word got round of her experience, the matron asked Jean to describe what had happened and subsequently told her that many other nurses had reported exactly the same thing.

STOCKSBRIDGE

There are many different classifications of ghost throughout the world, based on location, the type of phenomenon and the experiences of the people affected. These include poltergeists, doppelgangers (doubles), and a whole host of more traditional hauntings, such as grey ladies, monks, highwaymen, black dogs and so forth.

One other phenomenon, reported in several locations across Yorkshire as well as further afield, could be described as the 'road ghost'. This category includes such apparitions as phantom hitch-hikers who are picked up by motorists and promptly disappear from the confines of a locked car, ghost cars and other vehicles that appear from nowhere and sometimes cause crashes.

The Stocksbridge Bypass was opened in 1988 and for several years the many accidents on the new stretch of road – some fatal – were explained as being caused by driver error, bad street-lighting and faulty design of

Pearoyd Bridge follows the line of an ancient causeway.

the highway. That is, until one motorist came forward to tell of the figure in black, resembling a hooded monk, that had glided into the path of his car. But this was only the first of many reports of this strange figure dashing in front of vehicles, causing them to swerve erratically and often be involved in accidents.

A team of Sheffield bus inspectors, from the city's Mainline bus company, investigated the incidents and one of their number, bus inspector and medium Dave Williamson, claimed to have contacted the spirit of the monk and helped him to 'pass on'.

Reports still filter in from time to time, however, of a similar figure running across the roads on this busy seven-mile stretch of highway, so maybe it is time for the investigators to make a renewed approach.

Pearoyd Bridge originally formed part of an ancient causeway that was disrupted by the building of the Stocksbridge Bypass, and the ghostly children that have been reported in the area are another phenomenon connected with that road. Pat Heathcote was bewildered to watch a group of five or six boys and girls, dressed in old-fashioned pinafores and breeches, dancing together in a circle, as if around an invisible maypole, in a field above the new bridge. Barbara Lee, licensee of the Midhopestones Arms, also watched them from her window for several minutes and was amazed when they suddenly disappeared.

WORTLEY

At Christmas 1963 Mr G.M. Wood, of Huddersfield, and his brother were driving back from a party at Tankersley, a village between Sheffield and Barnsley. 'It was late at night,' Mr Wood told me, 'one of those beautiful, clear nights and the road was glistening with a fine, white frost.

'We had just negotiated the sharp 'S' bend around Wortley church on the A629 when a figure, which seemed to be dressed in black (the way a vicar might dress), suddenly appeared directly in front of the car. I immediately applied the brakes and skidded to a halt, but the figure had vanished and I was convinced he would be beneath the car. My brother and I nervously searched for the victim but he was nowhere to be seen. We looked all around the road and pavements but the figure had completely vanished!

'However, this was not the end of the matter. We never forgot the incident and spoke about it often over the years. Then, about thirty years later, I read in a national newspaper that, during the building of the Stocksbridge Bypass – the A616 – (about a quarter of a mile from our original experience) the construction team had refused to continue on account of the frequent appearances of a ghostly figure in a black monk-like garb!

Did these lanes near Wortley share the same spirit who was seen near the Stocksbridge bypass?

'I believe an exorcism service had to be held before work could recommence. Later, I read that research had discovered that a small monastery had existed in the area in the Middle Ages. I have no explanation for the above. I only know that our experience is etched into the memory of my brother and myself and we will never doubt that for some things there is no explanation.'

BEVERLEY

When former policeman Mally Talbot was running the Lady le Gros in Norwood Road he came to believe that a landlord from the late 19th century, Samuel Peacock, was haunting his pub. The ghost, who was seen by Sue, Mally's wife, appeared as an elderly Victorian gent who was wont to stride across the room and vanish through the fire escape. On one occasion, barman Andy Brown said he 'freaked out' after he heard footsteps

The former Lady le Gros pub, Beverley.

following him to the cellar of the bar. He then retraced his steps to find no one there. 'Sam', as the ghost was nicknamed, was not much of a nuisance and often helped Sue Talbot when she was cleaning. 'If I went towards a door with the vacuum cleaner, the door opened – and stayed open – to let me through. It didn't worry me at all,' she recalled.

* * *

The fireplace in the restaurant of the King's Head Hotel in Market Place is the centre of the paranormal activity at this inn. Landlord Paul Brooks said he couldn't believe his eyes one evening when he saw a man in a tweed suit leaning nonchalantly against it, only to disappear suddenly and without discernible movement.

The Kings Head Hotel, Beverley, stands on the site of the former Pack Horse Inn.

The ghost is believed to be a soldier who committed suicide in the stables of a pub that once stood on the site, the former Pack Horse Inn, and the restaurant of the King's Head is located where the stables used to be. Paul's wife Tricia has also seen the figure – once mistaking it for a customer who seemed to have been left behind when the pub was locked up that night. On another occasion she thought the man was one of the waiters, Andrew, and it wasn't until the ghost had disappeared that she remembered that Andrew had left two months previously!

One of the waitresses saw the man and thought he was waiting for a menu but in the second she turned round to get one for him and turned back, he had disappeared. She added that it sometimes felt cold and creepy in that area of the restaurant by the fireplace.

* * *

St Mary's Manor, Beverley.

In 1995 a pensioner, who had worked as a shorthand typist at St Mary's Manor in the 1940s, recalled a number of odd things that had occurred during her employment there.

At the time, the building housed the Royal Agricultural Executive Committee and, later, the Ministry of Agriculture, and the woman, who did not want to be named, said that the phenomena were usually connected with a small filing room at the rear of the manor. A colleague claimed to have seen a figure sitting on the edge of a nearby desk, even though no one had entered or left the room while she was working there. Another colleague, who held a séance in a panelled area near the filing room, suffered a choking fit, even though there was nothing wrong with her. 'She started making awful noises,' the typist remembered. 'I have never heard anything like them.' Her colleague said that during the sitting she had been contacted by a Chinese man, and was convinced that something had happened to him in that room.

* * *

In the 1980s the Mayor's Parlour, in the Beverley Guildhall, was reported to have been haunted by phantom footsteps, with all nine members of a building team experiencing the phenomenon.

The team had been told not to let anyone into the building as they had been carrying out dangerous demolition work, and yet they continually heard footsteps climbing the stairs and then walking across the floorboards of the Parlour. But, when foreman Mark Jordan and bricklayer Charles Carmichael went to investigate, they found no one who could have been responsible for the sounds.

Another member of the team, joiner Trevor Grundy, was the first to hear the footsteps when he began removing the flooring of the Mayor's Parlour. Mr Jordan also noticed the smell of strong cigar smoke on several occasions in the immediate vicinity, even though there was no one else close by – and certainly no one smoking a cigar.

The Guildhall, Beverley.

The most curious incident that happened to the team was during a tea break while they were listening to the radio. Said one of the men afterwards: 'The radio suddenly cut out and the heavy footsteps, more like a man than a woman, began crossing the first floor above us. When they had reached the other side of the room, the radio switched itself back on.'

The builders said they did not mind continuing the work, but always felt better when there was more than one of them in the building.

* * *

A number of shops in Beverley also have their ghostly residents.

Harvey's Pets, in Dyer Lane, seems to have a poltergeist that knocks things off the shelves. Manageress and owner Angela Harrison told the *Beverley Advertiser*: 'Dog beds have fallen off the shelves and packets of blades for cutting dogs' hair have also fallen down, along with worming tablets, which is odd as they are not stacked near the edge of the shelf.'

Mrs Margaret Middleton, Angela's mother, has also been disturbed by the antics. She was once aware of a rustling sound in the corner of the shop, accompanied by a strange shadow, but found no one there. 'We've nicknamed the ghost "George Milligan",' said Mrs Harrison, 'for no other reason than it seems to suit him. If anything falls off a shelf we always think George is around, but he's not a frightening ghost – just a friendly one.'

Just one incident has been reported next door in the Dove House Hospice charity shop, where muddy footprints were found in the middle of the carpet when the shop had been closed for the weekend. 'It was a bit of a puzzle,' said Rosemary Clark, the manageress. 'The carpet had been vacuumed on the Saturday when we closed up shop, and there was no corresponding line of footprints, leading away from the original two, giving any clue as to how they got there. Nothing ghostly has happened and it is tempting to think there is a rational explanation – but it remains a puzzle.'

The staff at the Beverley Bookshop have grown used to Horace, the nickname of this shop's ghost, and he is well liked. 'Some days we come in', reported Sally Middleton, 'and greetings cards are in the wrong place or, in the office, the bins appear to have been kicked over so there is rubbish strewn all over the floor, when the previous night it was left tidy. So we have come up with the phrase "Horace has been at it again!"'

The staff at Supa Snaps in Toll Gavel have come in first thing in the morning to find that photograph albums, which had been left neatly stacked the night before, had come off their shelves. Manageress Julie

Handley used to take tales of the shop being haunted with a pinch of salt until she started experiencing various odd happenings for herself. 'We think that this shop and Thornton's next door used to be a bakery owned by a Mr Adams who used to live here with his daughters,' she said. 'One of our staff members, who is a bit psychic, went up to a room in the top of the building and had a flashback. She saw three blonde-haired women whom we presume were the Adamses.'

Liz McGinley from Thornton's has corroborated what Ms Handley said, as she and her staff have experienced doors opening and closing by themselves and stock falling off shelves. 'Cardboard backings on chocolate displays were found on the floor,' she reported, 'while the chocolates remained undisturbed in their racks. Doors inside that were closed the night before could be open in the morning, but the alarms would not have been set off. We have nicknamed the ghost "George" and I always say good morning to him when I arrive for work but, although he is friendly, I do occasionally get a cold eerie chill down my back!'

In 1988 an army surplus store was the scene of ghostly activity, when owners Andrew and Yvonne Wood and business partner Tim Wood took over the premises. 'Heavy boxes that could not possibly fall off the shelves suddenly appear in the middle of the room,' said Andrew. 'If they had fallen they would have landed directly beneath the shelf – not yards away in the middle of the floor. It's just not possible. Really heavy motor-bike spares have also been moved from the shelves. If they had fallen they would have gone with a thump, but nothing has ever been damaged.

'Once an army helmet which was well secured to the wall came bounding across the floor. We were upstairs with a customer when we heard the bangs. The customer asked what it was and we told her it was only the ghost. She couldn't get out of the shop fast enough!'

Doors opened and closed by themselves, footsteps could be heard in the upstairs showroom when the place was empty and the shop's lights kept switching themselves on and off. Although neither Andrew, Yvonne nor Tim have ever seen the apparition believed to be responsible for the activity, the Woods' $2^1/_2$-year-old baby daughter, Jennifer, definitely noticed something from her pushchair. The young girl just sat there, looking past them on the shop floor, staring at the ceiling, and pointing and laughing.

'She was fascinated, but we couldn't see a thing,' said Yvonne. 'When we asked her what she could see she pointed to the ceiling, laughed to herself and said, "Look at the pretty lights." There was nothing there. It was really weird.'

* * *

The Cloisters Restaurant on Tiger Lane, built in 1730, stands amid a row of shops, though it was formerly a larger tavern, the Tiger Inn, until the 1840s, when business as a coaching inn dwindled and the building was subsequently sold and used for other purposes.

During the summer of 1982, a joiner was doing repair work on the staircase between the ground and first floors, and on one occasion his young apprentice looked up at the top of the staircase and saw the head and shoulders of a boy with fair hair and a scarf around his neck. But he was invisible below the waist.

During the period that the restaurant was a wine bar with the name 'Upstairs, Downstairs', the resident spook seemed to have a particular like – or dislike – for tradesmen such as joiners and bricklayers, its favourite trick being to tap them on the shoulder, upon which they would spin round to find no one there.

In the late 1970s the building used to be a motor-spares shop for Armstrong's garage just across the road, and many of the customers felt uneasy about entering the premises, particularly one man who refused to go anywhere near it, and sent colleagues to get parts for him, for he did not like the eerie atmosphere that he felt pervaded the ground floor.

There have been several occasions when the owners of today's restaurant have heard the eerie sound of something – or someone – being dragged across the first floor. The ghost may be a former resident of the Tiger Inn, though many of the interior furnishings of The Cloisters were salvaged from an old church in Hull, so it is possible that these days a vaporous vicar is flitting around the premises instead!

BRIDLINGTON

In 1998 a private house in Bessingby Road was reported in a local newspaper to have been haunted by a Victorian gentleman ever since the family moved there ten years before. The ghost had been witnessed not only by the family but also by visiting friends and neighbours.

A Victorian gentleman once haunted here!

An old photographic plate was found in the attic, left there by the previous owner, and this matched the description of the ghost. It was discovered to be a picture of one Harold Hill, a former occupant of the property. The family reported that they felt it was a comfort to have this ghost, because Mr Hill only appeared when there was trouble or when they were stressed or in a panic about something. It was as if he appeared in order to calm things down and to assure them that everything would be all right.

The range of phenomena over the years included a mystery whirlwind, which sent towels flying off the rails in the bathroom, and often the strong smell of tobacco throughout the house. However, one incident persuaded the family to call in an exorcist – when the pipe-smoking Mr Hill materialised in the guest bedroom one night and started to serenade a startled visitor. Former Bridlington vicar, the Reverend Tom Willis, an official exorcist, blessed every room in the house and yet the ghostly Mr Hill was said to continue in his capacity as a non-paying tenant.

DRIFFIELD

Successive tenants reported frightening happenings in a flat in Mill Street for several years. The most terrifying occurrence was the gas ring on the cooker turning itself on at night and pumping out lethal fumes. People simply forgetting to turn off the appliances may, of course, explain this, but the experiences of the tenant in November 1995, Tracey Mathison, were backed up by her predecessor, Beverley Tullock, who reported exactly the same thing.

The Reverend Tom Willis said that the occurrences sounded like the work of a poltergeist and if that were the case then a prayer or a blessing would probably cease the disturbances. However, he also pointed out that if an evil spirit was at work here, then an exorcism might be necessary to bring peace to the flat. With no follow-up report in the local papers, we can only assume that nothing more than a simple prayer was needed, and all apparently has returned to normal.

HULL

I n January 1998 a pantomime star had a spooky experience in the basement of Hull's New Theatre. Emma Morris, who played the title role in the theatre's production of *Dick Whittington*, saw the figure, dressed in a black cape and black top hat, as she walked down a narrow corridor and up a staircase, just seconds before she was due to make her entry on stage. She noticed that the air around her went freezing cold as the phantom brushed past.

Nicknamed 'Charlie' by staff members, the ghost – or perhaps there is more than one – has appeared in many different guises, including

The New Theatre, Hull.

as a grey hooded misty shape. The theories to account for the haunting range from a man who was stabbed in a fight in the 1840s, to someone who fell into the walls of the Assembly Rooms when they were being bricked up in the 19th century.

Sightings have been reported since the early part of the 20th century, the earliest modern report being from 1943 when theatre worker Eve Rainforth saw a figure in 'a dark grey riding coat, with long hair curling up at the ends.'

Alison Duncan, a spokesperson for the theatre, said she had not seen anything herself, but admitted that there had been numerous witnesses over the years. She explained that for many people Charlie was part of the theatre – part of the fixtures and fittings – but he remained a mystery to anyone who had yet to encounter him.

Dana, who appeared in the theatre's production of *Snow White* in 1982, often heard knocks on her dressing-room door while in the company of a wardrobe mistress, even though there was no one in the vicinity to account for them. She had also been followed by the sound of footsteps during her time at the theatre. House managers and cleaners have had many meetings with the spirit, including a cleaner, Jacqui Gower, who saw Charlie pulling himself a pint in the bar.

Possibly the most spectacular experience was that of city councillor Ann Stanley and her husband John, who both suddenly felt 'icy cold' while sitting in their box during a military band concert. Although her husband saw nothing, Mrs Stanley watched in amazement as a caped figure emerged out of a grey mist and then floated through the air, hovering four feet above people sitting in the stalls.

Mr Michael Lister, the current manager of the theatre, says: 'I have experienced Charlie on several occasions - twice in my office. The first occasion was before we had computers. I passed the door of my office and heard the sound of the electronic typewriter. I thought this was strange, as my assistant, Sylvia, was not due in to work for some time. On returning to my office several seconds later, the door was locked, as I had left it, with no sign of anyone. Some years later, after the computers had been installed, I passed the office door again and heard the sound of typing and also the sound of a bunch of keys jiggling and then dropping onto the desk. When I opened the locked door, there was no sign of Sylvia, but there was a message on the computer screen which read: "You have typed an invalid operation".'

* * *

In 1969 the *Hull Daily Mail* reported how a family living in a house in Argyle Terrace (now demolished although Argyle Street still exists) became the focus of attention for the spirit of a former occupant of the house.

Mr and Mrs Windley and their four children experienced sudden cold spots, strange noises such as bangs and crashes from empty rooms and being touched from behind by unseen hands. Numerous neighbours encountered the same things on their regular visits, and one girl saw what she described as the ghost of 'a very old lady dressed in a shawl and with long fingernails'.

This description matched that of a former owner, a Mrs Sellars, referred to in an anonymous letter sent to the family by a lady who had been her cleaner. The correspondent wrote that she had worked for Mrs Sellars more than fifty years previously and, having read a newspaper account of the family's troubles, recognised the description given by the young girl.

'Reading about your ghost has brought back memories to me,' she wrote, 'as I used to work at your house for a lady who was over eighty years old. I am well over sixty myself now, and was then a girl of fourteen. I used to clean up at your address. The old lady, Mrs Sellars, wore a shawl and was very tall and slim. She had no family and her husband died soon after they were married. She was a very religious person.'

MARKET WEIGHTON

I n 1993 Mr W.T. 'Nobby' Clarke attended a mini-reunion of ex-army buddies at the Half Moon in Market Weighton, run by his friend George Scorah.

Shortly after midnight, five or six of the group were still standing in the bar in a circle, pint pots in hand, when for some reason Nobby turned half-round and noticed a very healthy-looking, country-type gent sitting on the seat that ran along the back wall.

'Evening,' said Nobby, to which the man raised his glass and smiled, but did not speak. When Nobby turned back to the lads they were looking at him very strangely. 'How long has he been there?' he asked.

The Half Moon in Market Weighton.

His friends had not seen the man and, naturally, Nobby was subjected to the usual ridicule. George, however, who was clearing up behind the bar, was able to set his mind at rest. He called his wife, Marlene, who confirmed that she had noticed this chap on the seat on the back wall on a number of occasions – and yet no one else had … or has so far.

WATTON

A In June 1956 seven workmen had been contracted to help with the three-day sale of the furniture and fittings at Watton Abbey, as the owner had sold the property after thirty years of residency. The team were required to camp down on the ground floor of the abbey at night, ready for the next day's auction.

Watton Abbey.

At 1 am they were horrified to hear the tolling of the abbey's bell echoing through the ancient walls – but what scared them the most was that they knew the bell itself had been removed from the tower many years ago.

Grabbing their bedding they rushed from the abbey; one of the men was so afraid that he actually dived head first through a window, injuring himself as he fell into the garden. The foreman took his shotgun and fired the double-barrels skyward, upon which the tolling of the bell ceased immediately.

The work-team, unsurprisingly, then insisted on spending the rest of the night in the marquee on the lawn, which had been erected for the auctioning all too soon the following morning.

• Index •